LIV

MW01206428

A Deeper Look at the
Sacrament of the Holy Eucharist

by Christopher Lucas, OCSO

GETHSEMANI ABBEY, TRAPPIST, KY

PARACLETE PRESS
BREWSTER, MASSACHUSETTS

2016 First Printing

Living the Mass: A Deeper Look at the Sacrament of the Eucharist

Copyright © 2016 by The Abbey of Gethsemani

ISBN 978-1-61261-684-1

Paraclete Press name and logo (dove on cross) is a registered trademark of Paraclete Press, Inc.

Library of Congress Cataloging-in-Publication Data
Names: Lucas, Christopher, 1934- author.
Title: Living the mass : a deeper look at the sacrament of the Holy Eucharist
    / by Christopher Lucas, OCSO, Gethsemani Abbey, Trappist, Ky.
Description: Brewster MA : Paraclete Press Inc., 2016.
Identifiers: LCCN 2015049058 | ISBN 9781612616841
Subjects: LCSH: Lord's Supper—Catholic Church. | Mass. | Salvation—Catholic
    Church. | Paschal mystery. | Catholic Church—Doctrines.
Classification: LCC BX2215.3 .L83 2016 | DDC 234/.163—dc23
LC record available at http://lccn.loc.gov/2015049058

10 9 8 7 6 5 4 3 2 1

Published by Paraclete Press
Brewster, Massachusetts
www.paracletepress.com
Printed in the United States of America

CONTENTS

INTRODUCTION

"Those who lose their life for my sake will find it."
—Matthew 10:39

Self-Giving Love

Self-giving love is our greatest act, and without it we are nothing. Such love "makes" the person; that is, we transcend ourselves when, transformed by grace, we achieve this higher level of life, which we also call holiness. This love is the true source of happiness. Self-giving love is precisely what the paschal mystery and the Eucharist are all about.[1] God pours himself out to us in love and calls us to love in return, never stopping throughout eternity.

This book is about the Eucharist as the paschal mystery and how that affects us. Since the paschal mystery is the mystery by which we are saved, first we must ponder how salvation comes through it. Also, through the paschal mystery

[1] The term *mystery* is understood in this book as a reality or truth so rich in meaning that we cannot on earth fully understand it, and so it is always open to greater exploration.

we learn of God as the Trinity, for in it we see all three Divine Persons at work in the process of offering salvation. Thus, this book takes a Trinitarian approach.

WE ARE SAVED BY THIS LOVE

Christians believe that salvation comes through the death of Jesus by crucifixion. But how does the death of a man on a cross save us? How does Jesus's death bring life everlasting? How does it make us whole, as the word *salvation* implies?

Jesus's words and actions during his hidden life and public ministry were already leading toward salvation, because they anticipated the power of his paschal mystery.[2] But only in death was Jesus poured out for our salvation. Jesus *is* our salvation. Out of self-giving love he sacrificed himself to atone for our sins. Atonement is not appeasement of God, nor Jesus being punished in our place. Nor is it a payment to the devil to free us from his enslavement. Christ's death as sacrifice, his offering of his life to God, is an expression

2 *Catechism of the Catholic Church,* English translation for the United States of America, copyright 1994, United States Catholic Conference, Inc. Liberia Editrice Vaticiana, Ignatius Press, San Francisco, CA, #1115 (henceforth *CCC*).

of perfect obedience to the will of his Father. As an act of atonement, which means "at-*one*-ment," it is Christ making us one with God, in and through himself. Self-giving love is what has always mattered in Christian sacrifice.

IMPORTANCE OF THE PASCHAL MYSTERY

So, we are saved in response to the three Divine Persons giving us themselves in the paschal mystery—the passion, death, resurrection, and ascension of Jesus and the outpouring of the Holy Spirit at Pentecost. This divine self-giving is the very act of God being God; this act is not only revealed to us but also realized for us insofar as we live an authentic Christian life.

In the paschal mystery, the Father gives himself to us in his Son, abandons Jesus on the cross, and sends forth his Holy Spirit through Jesus. The Son, in doing the Father's will, suffers and dies, abandoned, and in death breathes forth the Holy Spirit. These are the roles of the three Divine Persons in the Trinity: the Father initiating, the Son responding, the Holy Spirit proceeding from the Father and the Son. Each one's personhood is realized in the unreserved gift of self, in loving communion.

Theologians call the mutual, loving self-giving of the Divine Persons to each other in the Blessed Trinity *circumincession*, which literally means "dancing around," as it were, in everlasting joy. That is how God is God, a community of love.

And love is what God is calling you and all his beloved people to in the paschal mystery. We become Godlike insofar as we give ourselves in love. Experience tells us that people become devout to the extent that they realize they are loved by God and called by that love to love in return.

For us, the paschal mystery is the most personal of all realities in our life. Nothing should be more intimate, more magnificent and important to you, for through it God is calling you to live by his divine love for all eternity in everlasting joy. Nothing deserves your attention and response more than this great mystery. You have already experienced it because all true human love is part of this self-giving love—requiring self-sacrifice that is a death to your false self and rebirth to your true self. This love is life-giving to you as well as to others.

Redeem the World

As a Christian, your calling is very great. You are called to redeem the world! "What?" you say. "Redeem the world? I thought Jesus did that and only he could do it." He did, but not completely. The truth is, out of incredible love for us, he left his work incomplete in order to give us a wonderful share in it. And that's where you come in. You must cooperate with Jesus in your own redemption and that of others. God calls us to intimate participation in this great work, especially through the paschal mystery in the sacrament of the Holy Eucharist. You are intimately involved in the Eucharistic work of redemption whether you realize it or not. This work means most importantly two great acts: worship of God and proclamation of the Gospel—all to the glory of God and the salvation of souls.

This book presents six different perspectives for understanding the Eucharist as the paschal mystery—six ways of understanding how we come to salvation. Each constitutes a chapter of the book. Each brings out different aspects of how we are affected through our participation in the Eucharist. All will show how, through the

Eucharist—as celebrated on our altars and as lived out in our everyday lives—we can most profoundly experience the paschal mystery and share that experience with others.

Chapter 7 explores how these perspectives are expressed through the Mass; and chapter 8, the final chapter, explains how they are reflected in the Mass as "the" remembrance of Jesus.

Chapter 1

PROCLAIMING THE WORD

"My God, my God, why have you forsaken me?"
—Matthew 27:46

Word Announced on Earth

At the Annunciation, God the Father announced his Word in human form. This was like a word being translated from one language into another, when the word remains unchanged in its meaning but takes on a new form and sound in its new language. In other words, Jesus, the eternal Word, did not change or leave the Godhead when he became man. He remained the Divine Word but also became a human Word.

But, as you know, a word loses something in translation. "[He] emptied himself, taking the form of a slave" (Phil. 2:7). In becoming man, the Word of God was emptied of his heavenly glory. The all-powerful, glorious Word was, as it were, only whispered on earth as a helpless infant in need of others for his well-being and even survival, joining the common lot of humankind.

Jesus lived a poor, humble, hidden life in Nazareth before he began his public ministry at about age thirty. He submitted to Mary and Joseph and to the laws of his time, including the Mosaic law. He lived "according to the flesh" (Rom. 9:5), a life of natural weakness along with all human creatures. He showed his humanity in his beautiful, very human compassion and pity for others, especially the lowly; he showed his divinity in his many miracles and marvelous teachings.

Yet, many did not accept Jesus. This rejection culminated in his death on the cross. It was the ultimate point of the *kenosis*, the emptying of the Word of God. Perhaps we could even say that, as rejected through his crucifixion, the Word-made-flesh was emptied of his very meaning, rejected even by God. This idea is supported by Jesus's cry on the cross, "My God, my God, why have you forsaken me?" (Matt. 27:46).

Many have puzzled over this cry of Jesus. Many deny it is a reaction to any real abandonment, treating it as a sort of delusion of a dying man.

Others say it is merely the first words of Psalm 22, which narrates the sufferings of a virtuous man and ends in a positive light. Of those who do take his cry literally, many see it as a response to the Father's wrath, renouncing Jesus and abandoning him to terrible suffering and death, perhaps in taking on the divine punishment for our sins. In this book we take his cry literally but in new and positive ways.

THE WORD RE-ANNOUNCED

Jesus's cry on the cross was undoubtedly a profound personal experience for him, but also it was a public event of the greatest importance. In it God the Father "gave him up for us all" (Rom. 8:32), not cutting him off in disdain, but rather releasing him as speakers do in sharing their words. Once spoken, a word cannot be unspoken; it is in a real sense abandoned to its hearer because the speaker lets it go and the hearer can accept or reject it. The Father was giving his Word to us in love as the pledge of our salvation. This abandonment by the Father was the great covenant-promise of salvation in which God literally gave us his Word. Here, the Word was re-announced; it was the re-Annunciation. It was the Gospel.

In his life on earth, Jesus revealed himself in a gradual and limited manner, but the paschal mystery was his full and complete revelation through the power of the Holy Spirit whereby all natural limitations were transcended. It was the greatest event of history. And it also transcended history.

The paschal mystery can and does affect people of all times and places, and it makes manifest unimagined realities. In it the early Church gradually began to realize the full nature of the Gospel, as the Church began to focus on Jesus himself. "The proclaimer became the proclaimed," as several theologians have put it. More than the message about Christ or the message Christ preached, the Gospel came to be understood as, above all, Christ himself, the Word preached forth from the cross as the "word of the cross" (1 Cor. 1:18 ESV).

JESUS REBORN

Jesus was reborn through the baptism of the cross into the realm of the divine. His humanity was divinized. He was resurrected as the mystical Christ. As risen, Christ could appear and disappear anywhere and anytime, pass through closed doors and so on, as we see in the Gospel accounts of the Resurrection. All this mirrors what Jesus is as the second person of the Trinity. The Father is ever begetting his Son in the everlasting now of eternity, an eternal rebirth.

By abandoning Jesus to his death on the cross, he was giving Jesus rebirth. This is mirrored in human birth. A child being born experiences its birth as a death, as being cast out from the only world it knows, abandoned by its mother.

This reborn Christ, the "firstborn from the dead" (Col. 1:18; Rev. 1:5), became a "life-giving spirit" (1 Cor. 15:45), the Word of God proclaimed by the Father to give us our supernatural life. Moreover, Jesus proclaimed himself. He laid down his life to take it up again anew in a glorious way, as he declared, "For this reason the Father loves me, because I lay down my life in order to take it up again" (John 10:17). What the Father and Jesus did, they did together. The abandonment was a mutual act of re-announcing. And what they do mutually is through their Holy Spirit. At his death, Jesus cried out, "Father, into your hands I commit my spirit" (Luke 23:46 ESV). The translated human Word re-announced himself as the mystical Word of salvation by his abandonment to the Father. With the Father, he thus breathed forth the Holy Spirit in his sigh of death.

THE RESOUNDING HOLY SPIRIT

So, can you see that the paschal mystery is the mystery of the Son abandoning himself to the Father and being resurrected by the Father, not only as an event in history, but transcending history into the eternal now—the Son ever being born through the Father's self-giving in the unity of the Holy Spirit? Jesus is "the Resurrection" (John 11:25), ever rising up to life, ever being reborn.

Here we can see the Holy Spirit as the Sound of the Word. The reborn Christ comes to us through the Holy Spirit as a word comes through its sound. The Holy Spirit is the divine *Pneuma*, the vibrant Breath of God. Modern science tells us that sound is the vibration of air. God is like us: we first think a word, and then we say it. The Divine Mind thinks the Word and puts it into Sound. [3]

Traditionally, the Resurrection has been seen as birth into a new life that Jesus did not have in his bodily humanity, a kind of life that was immortal and belonged to the divine, mystical order. St. Paul, in Romans 6:10, said that Jesus's life is a life in God. At the Annunciation, the Father announced the Word in the flesh, into material reality. At the paschal mystery, the Father re-announced the Word in the spirit. The first announcement was in and through the Virgin Mary; the second is in and through each soul that embraces Jesus in faith.

PROCLAMATION EVOKES FAITH

We hear and embrace God's proclaimed Word by faith. Faith is taking God's Word for it. When we do not understand something someone tells

---

3 Possible evidence in Holy Scripture for seeing the Holy Spirit as Sound: At the creation the Holy Spirit hovered over the waters as a sound hovers over a room (Gen 1:2); the Holy Spirit is often referred to as poured out as a sound is poured out (Acts 2:17-18; 10:45; Titus 3:6; Rom. 5:5); at Pentecost a powerful sound was heard at the coming of the Holy Spirit (Acts 2:1-4); on being born of the Spirit Jesus said, "the wind blows where it chooses and you hear the sound of it" (John 3:8).

us yet accept it, we are making an act of faith, accepting something as true on the authority of another. The lofty Word of God is infinitely beyond our unaided ability to comprehend, so faith is the only way we can receive Jesus. And what a great gift! By faith we receive the infinite Word of God.

Faith is accepting Jesus into one's heart, providing a temple, a dwelling place, for the risen mystical Christ as our true life. The author of the Letter to the Ephesians prays "that Christ may dwell in your hearts through faith" (Eph. 3:17). In Holy Scripture, the heart refers to the core of our being. That is where Jesus yearns to be.

All of what we have covered so far in this chapter leads us now to explore how the Eucharist is the ongoing paschal mystery. The Council Fathers of Vatican II tell us that Jesus instituted the Eucharist "to perpetuate the sacrifice of the cross" (*Sacrosanctum Concilium,* 47). In each of the four Eucharistic Prayers, right after the consecration the priest declares, "The mystery of faith," and the congregation responds by proclaiming Jesus's death. As we have claimed, that death *is* the proclamation of the Word, the Father speaking the Word forth as the "word of the cross" (1 Cor. 1:18 ESV), the salvific Gospel.

We read in the *Catechism of the Catholic Church*:

> The Eucharist is thus a sacrifice because it *re-presents* (makes present) the sacrifice of the cross, because it is its *memorial* and because it *applies* its fruit: [Christ], our Lord and God, was once and for all to offer himself to God the Father by his death on the altar of the cross, to accomplish there an everlasting redemption. But because his priesthood was not to end with his death, at the Last Supper "on the night when he was betrayed," [he wanted] to leave to his beloved spouse the Church a visible sacrifice (as the nature of man demands) by which the bloody sacrifice which he was to accomplish once and for all on the cross would be re-presented, its memory perpetuated unto the end of the world, and its salutary power be applied to the forgiveness of sins we daily commit. (*CCC*, 1366)

ACTIVE AND PASSIVE PARTICIPATION

We participate at Mass actively and passively, consciously and subconsciously. In fact, the most important realities happen beyond our consciousness in our deepest depths, in the very core of our being.

We "hear Mass," passively listening to the priest say the Mass, give the homily, and so on, but on a higher spiritual plane we hear God's Word. At Mass, the Father abandons his Word, Jesus, to us. It is the "mystery of faith," the very source of faith that "comes from what is heard" (Rom. 10:17), whereby we have Christ living in our hearts. We experience this profound reality not on the conscious level but in the core of our being, what has been called the supraconscious. So at every Mass we are strengthened in faith and come to a deeper, closer union with Jesus. Even more, in our active participation we proclaim not merely human words but Jesus himself as the Word; we "proclaim Christ crucified" (1 Cor. 1:23). We do this as a Christian community and individually by virtue of our baptismal priesthood. That is the real heart of evangelization—we proclaim to the world what is its greatest need: Jesus, its Savior.

When Jesus cried out in Aramaic, *Eli, Eli, lema sabachthani?*—"My God, my God, why have you forsaken me?"—he was utterly misunderstood by those who responded: "This man is calling for Elijah" (Matt. 27:46–47). Even today, many people hearing the proclaimed Word of the Gospel misunderstand it because their hearts are not truly open. But when we receive the Word in obedient faith, he touches our inmost being: "All of us, with unveiled faces, seeing the glory of the Lord as though reflected in a mirror, are being transformed into the same image from one degree of glory to another; for this comes from the Lord, the Spirit" (2 Cor. 3:18).

OUR TRUE VOCATION

This treasure of the Word is a gift and call to proclaim Christ at Mass and throughout our Christian life insofar as we are transformed in Christ, re-created in the image of the Word. That last statement is very important. Our transformation in Christ must be ongoing, not confined to the one-hour ritual celebration of the Mass on Sundays. We must make our whole life a "sacrifice of the Mass" through self-giving love. The Church urges the faithful to "live out the meaning of what they hear, contemplate, and do in the celebration" (*CCC*, 1101). Indeed, the Mass sends us out on our life mission of receiving and proclaiming Jesus; as the old Latin Mass put it, *Ite, missa est*—"Go, you are sent forth."

The sacrament of the Holy Eucharist is not simply a remembrance of a past event or an effect of Christ's past redemptive action; it is the saving event itself, which ever exists in its eternal, supernatural aspect for the ongoing redemption of the world. Through the Mass, we are intimately involved as the "work of our redemption is carried on" (*Lumen Gentium,* 3).

Jesus himself told us, "I am the way, and the truth, and the life" (John 14:6); thus, we must live Christ. He is our true vocation, our true way of life. He is the call. We hear this great call not just once but throughout our lifetime. God calls us again and again, from grace to grace, from holiness to holiness.

So, you see, God is calling you to live Christ and to share with him the great work of the redemption of the world. There is no greater work.

Chapter 2

RELEASING POWER

"Christ [is] the power of God."
—1 Corinthians 1:24

The Big Bang

The paschal mystery was the big bang[4] of the new creation, the explosion of infinite, divine, life-giving love. It was God's bestowing eternal life upon his people, establishing the kingdom of God in power. "So if anyone is in Christ, there is a new creation" (2 Cor. 5:17). From the cross, God the Father was releasing the infinite power of his divine-human Word in the form of energy we call divine grace. This power or grace transcends time and space and extends out to all persons of all times and places. This power is also referred to as the "power of his resurrection" (Phil. 3:10), since the

---

4 Scientists explain that the term "big bang" refers not to a physical explosion but, more precisely, to an emergence.

Cross and the Resurrection are part of the one great paschal mystery. Pope Francis has told us: "Christ's resurrection is not an event of the past; it contains a vital power that has permeated this world."[5]

Jesus saw his messianic power as bringing on the new age foretold by the prophets in which the Holy Spirit would be poured out upon all flesh. However, Jesus's power was not fully exercised until his "hour" had come, the hour of his paschal mystery. Through his resurrection, Jesus received the fullness of power in heaven and on earth. That was when he was designated Lord and Messiah.

Through the sacrament of the Holy Eucharist, the big bang explosion of the new creation is still going on, far exceeding the old creation. Indeed, the very purpose of creation is to lead to the coming of a "new heaven and a new earth" (Rev. 21:1). This kingdom of God, being above all a matter of self-giving love—the love which endures always—will flourish forever.

SOURCE AND SUMMIT

The power of the new creation is still with us today, especially in the sacraments and above all

5 *Evangelii Gaudium: Apostolic Exhortation* # 276, cited in *Origins* 43, no. 27, December 5, 2013.

in the sacrament of the Eucharist, the sacrament of sacraments. The *Catechism* explains: "The Eucharist is 'the source and summit of the Christian life.' The other sacraments, and indeed all ecclesiastical ministries and works of the apostolate, are bound up with the Eucharist and are oriented towards it. For in the blessed Eucharist is contained the whole spiritual good of the Church, namely Christ himself, our Pasch" (*CCC,* 1324).

That is the key: the Holy Eucharist contains Jesus himself. Jesus is the great sign or sacrament because his glorified risen humanity reflects what he is in the Trinity—that is, the Image of God. He is the abundant life you first received at your baptism and continue to receive in the sacrament of the Eucharist. The Eucharist is the "mystery of faith" that strengthens your faith deep in the core of your being.

Remember the definition of a sacrament from your old catechism? It went something like this: "A sacrament is an efficacious sign instituted by Christ to give grace." It said an *efficacious* sign— not just a road sign, but a sign that brings about what it signifies. We now see that a sacrament is able to be efficacious because it carries the power of Christ.

SACRAMENTS EMPOWER US

Above all this Eucharistic power is life-giving power. Jesus became a "life-giving spirit" (1 Cor. 15:45) through his paschal mystery. The Eucharist is an explosion of life-giving love, the transcendent life of Christ shared with us. In this sacrament, we experience a new birth. "Blessed be the God and Father of our Lord Jesus Christ! By his great mercy he has given us a new birth into a living hope through the resurrection of Jesus Christ from the dead" (1 Pet. 1:3). This new birth is spiritual birth in union with the risen Christ: "Anyone united to the Lord becomes one spirit with him" (1 Cor. 6:17). Through the Eucharist you are evermore becoming the "new [person] created in justice and holiness of truth" (Paul VI, *Gravissimum Educationis*, intro. 2).

By the great outpouring of divine love, God has made us his own beloved children, sons and daughters of God with the Son of God. In this way, God is establishing his kingdom on earth, the kingdom of his beloved people elevated to superabundant life with God.

The sacraments, especially the Eucharist, empower us with the grace of Christ, which is first of all Christ himself. In our union with him, we are being transformed into his likeness. Theologians call this transformation sanctifying grace—our being sanctified through, with, and in Jesus. We distort ourselves by our sins, but by grace we are restored to the divine image, for "where sin increased, grace abounded all the more" (Rom. 5:20).

The power of the Eucharist increases in us sanctifying grace and the virtues. Sanctifying grace is a habit that affects our nature. A virtue is a habit that affects our faculties. In short, we become Christlike in our being (grace) and in our actions (virtues). These good habits enable us to attain the true end of our nature: to be who we are called to be—that is, united with the Lord.

THE POWER OF VIRTUE

The true power of the human person is virtue. The word itself comes from the Latin *virtus*, which signifies strength and power. As graced by

God, we are empowered to live a virtuous life, which is what we mean when we say, "Live the Mass." It is by grace and virtue that we are one with Jesus in redeeming the world.

The power of the Eucharistic paschal mystery is realized in these virtues that the Holy Spirit infuses into our hearts. An infusion is a breathing in. The Holy Spirit, the Breath of God, breathes these marvelous powers into our soul, like the mighty wind that shook the house at Pentecost and fired up the disciples. In this way, the Holy Spirit builds up the People of God, the Church.

We express God's grace especially in the great virtues of faith, hope, and love, which are called the theological virtues because they cannot be achieved except through God's infusing them. These are the Holy Spirit's divinizing effects on our three greatest faculties: intellect (*faith*), memory (*hope*), and will (*love*). Together with the gifts of the Holy Spirit—wisdom, knowledge, understanding, counsel, piety, fortitude, and fear of the Lord—the theological virtues order our moral and religious acts, enabling us to respond rapidly and faithfully to the inspirations of the

Divine Spirit. All of these blessings are God's power bestowed upon us.

On the more immediately practical level of our spiritual life, the sacraments give us the graces we need to keep God's commandments, for our own good. When our modern gurus tell us how to be happy, they tell us that first and foremost we must have good relationships. When you think about it, this points us right to the Commandments, for they are all about having good relationships! So, to be happy, keep the Commandments. They are God telling us to be happy, and telling us how.

Christ's gift of salvation, given through his Holy Spirit, offers us the powerful graces necessary to persevere and grow in the virtues. This growth in virtue in turn enhances our freedom and ability to overcome evil and do good works—in short, to live Christ.

Every so often, some popular magazine has an article on powerful people, but it always misses the point by focusing exclusively on this-worldly power. Virtues are far greater powers than any earthly ones. They are above all supernatural powers, which have consequences not only in this world but also in the next. They are personal powers involving your very personhood and your destiny. They are the transformation of your very being; they make you what you are.

PRACTICING VIRTUE

Developing virtue is difficult. But as one grows, the difficulty diminishes; and the more solidly we possess virtues, the more we are masters of ourselves and can do what is right and good with ease and enjoyment. More importantly, virtues dispose us to be in communion with divine love, with God's holy will—that is, with your vocation, the object of your life and of your truest and deepest desires. In this divine love, you are in union with the risen mystical Christ in redeeming the world. No one is an island; your life affects others—and so often in ways you cannot see!

We rarely experience the theological virtues directly but instead encounter them through more mundane little virtues. We could call the virtues we exercise in our everyday keeping of God's commandments—patience, kindness, generosity, and gentleness—great little virtues. They are little in that they're not revered in the same way as "big" virtues such as courage, daring, knowledge of the world, cleverness, and worldly prudence. Yet, they are great because they are gifts of the Divine Spirit, because their cultivation requires much effort, and because with them we can accomplish great things.

St. Benedict in his holy Rule goes so far as to tell his monks that it is through the everyday "little" virtue of patience that they share in the redemptive sufferings of Christ. He sees his monks' "good zeal" as respect, patience, and obedience toward one another. Such "little" virtues arise daily and thus provide practical and frequent opportunities to do good and please God. Little things done often are actually big things. We have only to think of the "little way" of sanctity of St. Thérèse of Lisieux.

It is critical in view of the many evils of our day that we live the Mass by practicing virtues—big ones and little ones. Our society needs virtuous people. The fact that by our own power we can only practice them imperfectly is no excuse for not trying; we need only to put our trust in our merciful God. How the Father delights in seeing us grow in virtue, in the likeness of his divine Son!

Chapter 3

OVERCOMING SIN

*"For our sake [God] made [Jesus] to be sin who
knew no sin."*

—2 Corinthians 5:21

Our Sinful Condition

As we have noted, the Catholic
Church teaches that Jesus instituted
the sacrament of the Eucharist to
perpetuate the sacrifice of the Cross. Through that
sacrifice, sin was overcome. In this chapter we
will look at our sinful condition, the nature of sin,
God's response to sin, and our response to God.

In the book of Genesis we learn that God made
Adam and Eve right—even in his own image and
likeness. They walked with God as his intimate
friends and enjoyed his many blessings. But
by sinning, they put themselves in the wrong,
resulting in their trying to hide from God, for
they had made themselves his enemies. God had

forbidden Adam and Eve to eat of the tree in the center of the garden, but they disobeyed. They broke God's word; they sinned.

Moreover, by sinning they had distorted their own being and were no longer recognizable as God's most wonderful creation on earth. So we read: "But the LORD God called to the man, and said to him, 'Where are you?'" (Gen. 3:9).

Whether or not we take this story literally, the point is that Adam and Eve are representative of each of us; each of us experiences something of their original wrongness in our weakness and inclination to sin. And we all have sinned and made ourselves enemies of God.

In today's moral climate, sin is often trivialized; it is covered up, or called simply a mistake. We are told, "Just do it," "Sex is fun," "Greed is good," "It's just being natural." Around the world, morality is still an eye for an eye: "You hurt me, and I'll hurt you back." It's a "get even" mentality far from Christian morality.

Sin is an offense against God. It damages our relationship with God and puts us in the wrong. The wrongness of sin is more than intellectual wrongness, and more even than moral wrongness, as that is commonly understood. It is essentially and most profoundly an existential and ontological wrongness, because sin distorts our very nature and existence. Sin disrupts the order set up by God. In revolting against God, Adam and Eve revolted against themselves, their nature, and the nature of creation as established by God. Nature, in turn, has revolted against human nature. A whole chain of disorders is set up because of sin. It is far more profound than anything we can consciously experience or realize.

God's Dealing with Sin

Because it is such an abominable evil, sin arouses the dreadful wrath of God's judgment. God explodes with his angry Word. He declares it loud and clear, in full power. Could we even say that God becomes so angry that he utters his Word as a curse word, as we read in the Letter to the Galatians, "Christ redeemed us from the curse of the law by becoming a curse for us—for it is written, 'Cursed is everyone who hangs on a tree'" (Gal. 3:13)?

Obviously this is anthropomorphism. God is not a human being. Authors of the Bible, in trying to convey what is ineffable, often attributed to God human attitudes, feelings, and actions. Nevertheless, in telling us about the wrath of God, they point to something even more important: God's loving care for his people. To attribute love to God is surely no anthropomorphism, for "God is love" (1 John 4:16) and human love is but a pale image of God's supreme love.

God becomes angry because he cares. When one does not care, the response is apathy. The Bible calls God "angry" in order to depict his great concern for the horrible state we put ourselves into when we sin. This anger reveals his disappointment because he expects great things of us. "God's wrath" consists of unrepentant sinners experiencing the consequences of their sins; it is God's wake-up call to repentance and cure. His angry Word is nonetheless his own Divine Word, his Son. Into the very depths of the horrible state of our human wrongness and brokenness, God sent his own Son to get us out of it.

We will be able to understand this fully only when we are in heaven; only then will we be able to grasp the full horror of sin and the merciful way God saves us from it. We see sin manifested most profoundly in the wounded, broken body of the Crucified One.

JESUS MADE SIN

The Cross was not the condemnation of sinners; it was the condemnation of sin itself. Sin was conquered through the Cross; it was in and through Christ that sin was condemned. St. Paul told us how this condemnation took place when he declared: "For our sake [God] made [Jesus] to be sin who knew no sin" (2 Cor. 5:21).

What a statement: Jesus was made to be sin! *God* did it! And for *our* sake! *The New International Commentary on the New Testament* says there is "no sentence more profound in the whole of Scripture."[6] But how can we comprehend this statement? Many Bible commentaries simply bypass it or water it down. Yet, we can start by contemplating the crucified, broken body of Christ experienced in our Eucharist. Since Christianity's earliest days, the Eucharist has been referred to

---

6 *The New International Commentary on the New Testament*, General Editor F.F. Bruce. "Paul's Second Letter to the Corinthians", by Philip Edgumbe Hughes, Th.D., D. Litt., (Grand Rapids, Mi, Wm. B. Eerdmans, Seventh printing January 1979), 211.

as the *Breaking of Bread*. At the Eucharist, Christ is present as at Calvary because the Eucharist perpetuates the sacrifice of the Cross.

On Calvary, Jesus was "made sin" by his brokenness in his passion. To sin is to break God's word. This is true with regard to God's word as his laws and commands. But it is true above all in the personal Word of God, Jesus himself. Thus, we can see sin as the broken Word of God. The crucified, broken Jesus is the Christ "made sin."

This is not to say that God committed sin. The idea that God offended himself makes no sense. We need to remember that Jesus died as man and not as God, for it was the Word as translated into human form that was broken on Calvary. Jesus became human sin, and through his broken body he healed us of our sins: "by his wounds you have been healed" (1 Pet. 2:24).

THE REPARATION OF SIN

Jesus did not remain broken; he was resurrected from the dead. The risen Jesus is the "reparation" of sin—in the sense of brokenness repaired—and thus he was no longer sin. By dying he suffered sin's brokenness in his own human nature, then by rising from the dead his human nature was repaired and uplifted to a new level of reality. He is the "new humanity" (Eph. 2:15), the "firstborn from the dead" (Col. 1:18; cf. Rev. 1:5). He is the divine-human Word who, in offering himself, offers perfect satisfaction for all offenses against God, because he is the perfect Word of reparation. At Mass we offer to the Father that perfect Word of reparation.

This repair has momentous effects for us, for Jesus assumed *all* our sins when he was made sin. All brokenness due to sin is repaired in the risen Christ, as we read: "If Christ has not been raised, your faith is futile and you are still in your sins" (1 Cor. 15:17).

God's Word uttered as a curse is also his Word of salvation. From the viewpoint of sin, his Word is a curse; from the viewpoint of salvation, it is a blessing. "For by the same means by which you punished our enemies you called us to yourself and glorified us" (Wis. 18:8). God's repaired Word overcomes sin and brings his people to the glory of salvation. The crucified and risen Jesus as "payment" offered to God more than satisfies for all human sins.

As you know, the traditional argument goes something like this: human nature sinned and must make reparation to be redeemed. Christ was given a human nature for this purpose, with his divine nature providing infinite redemptive value. Only the God-man could save us. Thus St. Paul tells us that Christ is our redemption—to be redeemed we must be one with Christ.

This reparation is no isolated event, nor does it involve only Christ; it affects all of creation: "Through him God was pleased to reconcile to himself all things" (Col 1:20). Jesus is the atonement of sin, the "at-*one*-ment" who is gathering together all repentant sinners into one. In and through him is the reconciliation of the world to God. All the baptized form one new mystical person with Christ.

OUR REDEMPTION THROUGH CHRIST

All of this significantly involves us. We read in the Letter to the Ephesians, "[God,] even when we were dead through our trespasses, made us alive together with Christ . . . and raised us up with him" (Eph. 2:5–6). Jesus's resurrection involves us because the Father has given us life by raising up Christ to be our very life; Jesus Christ is "the resurrection and the life" (John 11:25). Thus does St. Paul argue: "If, because of one man's trespass, death exercised dominion through that one, much more surely will those who receive the abundance of grace and the free gift of righteousness exercise dominion in life through the one man, Jesus Christ" (Rom. 5:17; cf. Rom. 4:25).

Our redemption comes through Christ; it is not our doing, although we must cooperate in it. Christians of all denominations agree that redemption was the work of Jesus's paschal mystery. The proclamation of the Word at Mass, which we receive in faith, makes us right, justified, holy: "since we are justified by faith, we have peace with God through our Lord Jesus Christ" (Rom. 5:1 ESV). The Eucharist effects our ongoing justification as the great "mystery of faith." And so, St. Paul's enigmatic statement, "For our sake [God] made [Jesus] to be sin who knew no sin," continues: "so that in him we might become the righteousness of God" (2 Cor. 5:21).

As we have noted, faith is taking God's Word for it. We exercise faith at Mass by embracing

Jesus in our heart so that he can be our true life. We conform ourselves to God's Word, whom we accept as the ultimate Truth of reality. Although we cannot fully understand this infinitely lofty divine-human Word of God, the Word edifies us, transforming the soul into the divine image through sanctifying grace— like a dark, blurry, unrecognizable photo being made bright, fully clear, and sharp through its developing solutions. Now God does not cry out to us as he did to Adam: "Where are you?" (Gen. 3:9).

To repentant souls, God's powerful Word is experienced as the redeeming Word of love and mercy embraced by faith. But that same Word is experienced as terrible wrath by the unrepentant, because they hold on to their sin and in their unbelief are one with it in slavery. Pope Francis tells us, "God judges us by loving us. If I embrace his love then I am saved, if I refuse it, then I am condemned, not by him, but by my own self, because God never condemns, he only loves and saves."[7]

---

7 Pope Francis, "Way of the Cross at the Colosseum," March 20, 2013, in *L'Osservatore Romano*, no. 14, Wednesday, 3 April 2013.

So, to say that Christ's brokenness was repaired at his resurrection and that this was therefore the reparation of sin is not to say that all sin was thus annihilated, as if sin were some abstract reality. On the contrary, because sin exists only in us as concrete individuals, it is only in us that sin is annihilated, through God's merciful forgiveness applied in a personal way. It is through the grace of the Word received in faith that salvation achieves its purpose. The reality of Christ's passion and death must be applied to individuals in order for them to be saved. In his great redemptive love for us, Jesus has identified himself with all humankind in his Mystical Body. Thus, his brokenness is still being repaired in us, in the repair of our souls through our repentance and faith.

All of this happens at Mass as the work of redemption is carried out through the Eucharist. Redemption is ongoing as God forgives sins when we repent sincerely. The wonderful sacrament of reconciliation follows from the Eucharist for this purpose.

THE TINIEST SEED

If your faith was challenged at seeing that God made Jesus to be sin, look again. It is by his being made sin that we have faith at all! For us to become holy through faith, God had to break down his Word so we could receive it, "so that in him we might become the righteousness of God" (2 Cor. 5:21). Now we begin to see the significance of the Eucharistic *Breaking of Bread*.

So, paradoxically, God made it possible for us to have faith when he made Jesus to be sin. It is only by God's breaking down his lofty Word of Truth in love that we are able to receive it. Through his great love for us, God made his Word into the tiniest seed of life, like a mustard seed. He made his Word the simplest truth, so easy to conceive, and yet full of life-giving power of love and mercy with which to conquer the world.

In this context, the Word of God is still broken. Jesus, even as resurrected, still has his wounds, and Jesus is forever dead to the life he lived on earth before his resurrection. For each individual Jesus came to save, he is still "made sin," still in need of repair through each individual sinner's receiving him in repentance and faith. Jesus accepts us in our brokenness; we need to accept him in his, and recognize him in our broken fellow men and women. Through the Eucharist as the *Breaking of Bread*, we experience Christ made sin; we personally experience Christ made *our* sins to take them away.

Jesus is beyond all limits of time and space. He is at once whole and broken. His fullness is in the tiny host or drop of blood in the chalice received at Holy Communion. Through the miracle of the Eucharist, you receive the whole Christ. Holy Scripture testifies to this simultaneous wholeness and brokenness. For example, in the book of Revelation 5:6–14 Jesus is presented in heaven as the slain Paschal Lamb, but he stands like one who has conquered. As John the Baptist declared: "Here is the Lamb of God who takes away the sin of the world!" (John 1:29).

The brokenness of the crucified Christ has profound effects on Jesus and all souls. Our subsequent three chapters will bear this out.

Chapter 4

OPENING THE WAY

"I am the way."

—JOHN 14:6

JESUS THE OPEN WAY

Jesus was broken in body and soul at his death. We can see this as the opening of the way of salvation. At his death Jesus's body and soul separated like a double gate opening wide; he said, "I am the gate" (John 10:7–9). We enter through that open gate at baptism; we are incorporated into Christ, who is our salvation.

By abandoning Jesus to his death, the Father was opening the Way wide even for the worst of sinners to obtain pardon and be saved. Now all can be saved, in and through Christ. Indeed, so wonderful is this great mystery that every wound of the Crucified One is an opening of the way of salvation: "By his wounds you have been healed" (1 Pet. 2:24; cf. Isa. 53:5).

Jesus dies no more, for he is forever dead to the life he lived on earth before his paschal mystery. He rose to a new life that transcends this world; he became a life-giving spirit. Yet, as such, the Lord still has his wounds for us. Thus, he is forever the open gate, the Way wide open for all to enter who will.

The Eucharist as paschal mystery must be lived. We must make our whole life a "holy sacrifice of the Mass." Baptism gives us a right and duty to live the Eucharistic paschal mystery. In a mystical sense,[8] throughout our baptismal life—in our prayer, sacrifices, sufferings, and good works—we advance in ways of salvation and holiness through the open wounds of Jesus.

Jesus is the Way to follow, not only in his teachings, but especially in his example. In seeking to conform to his image, we must endeavor to practice the virtues he did. Christian tradition tells us that the way to attain sanctity is to imitate Christ.

---

8 All the baptized have a mystical life insofar as they are members of Christ's Mystical Body, the Church. This does not mean all are mystics in the sense of having unusual mystical experiences.

HUMAN NATURE: A CROSS

The first step in imitating Christ is desire. But to fulfill that desire we must follow Christ to the Cross. That is where following him leads, as Jesus said, "And I, when I am lifted up [on the cross] from the earth, will draw all people to myself" (John 12:32). And that is our place when we are at Mass: with Christ at the Cross.

Everyone experiences being drawn toward the Eucharist in the deepest depths of their being, for no one escapes the cross. Our human nature is a cross: one beam running contrary to another, the horizontal flesh against the vertical spirit: "For what the flesh desires is opposed to the Spirit, and what the Spirit desires is opposed to the flesh" (Gal. 5:17).

The cross is the symbol of contradiction, and human nature is contradictory. When you think about this, you will realize it is true from your own experience.

We are a cross because we are born into a world that is a cross with its many contradictions, conflicts, and enticements to sin. To the extent that we conform to the world,[9] we experience an

---

9 *World* here means the world disordered due to the influence of evil spirits and to the sins of humankind, from Adam and Eve to our own day.

existential scattering of our life and being. Our deepest desires are affected by this scattering, even from infancy.

FOURFOLD TENDENCIES

Our most basic tendencies are rooted in the instinctive levels of our being. On the horizontal level are the instincts for pleasure and possessiveness; on the vertical level are the instincts for social relations and self-preservation. The downward tendency, the self-preservation instinct, is our strongest—the longest beam of the cross. Our weakest tendency is our upward movement to transcend self and go out to others, the social instinct—the shortest beam.

These natural dispositions are good in themselves, but due to the weakness of our human nature (Catholics would be inclined to say our "fallen nature," referencing original sin), they are out of order. Consequently, as the world attracts us, we experience strong inclinations to go to excess. If these instincts are held in proper order and within due limits, all is well, but if not, they will get us into trouble and enslave us. We all know this danger by experience.

At the level of instincts there is no sin, but at the moral level we are responsible for what we do. When we sin, it is a great slavery. Our most important freedom is freedom from sin, which can taint even our deepest hopes and desires. To become like Jesus, we need to be opened and set free from our excessive proclivities. Paradoxically, our freedom comes from nailing ourselves to the cross of this world with Christ: "And those who belong to Christ Jesus have crucified the flesh with its passions and desires" (Gal. 5:24). Our unruly passions and desires need to be restrained and ordered by a mystical crucifixion with Christ. We must be able to say with St. Paul, "I have been crucified with Christ" (Gal. 2:19). We need in this way to die to ourselves and to live for Jesus. Death to self means dying daily to our distorted desires, our excessive cravings for pleasure, possessions, self-concern. To be "crucified with Christ" is to make one's life a "holy sacrifice of the Mass."

Nailed to the Cross

This holy sacrifice means real sacrifice. We need to hammer in spiritual nails of self-denial by which we restrain the inordinate tendencies of our being. By these nails we say "nay" to "all" these destructive drives, so that we may be "crucified . . . to the world" (Gal. 6:14) with Christ. The nails in the hands save us from inordinately going out after pleasures on one side and possessions on the other; the nail through the feet saves us from going down after excessive self-concern, self-glorification, and pride.

On the religious level, these nails are the virtues of chastity, poverty, and obedience. They are great gifts from God. We first encountered them at our baptism, where we were "crucified with [Christ]" (Rom. 6:6). Through our sponsors, we said "nay" to "all" temptations of the devil (through obedience), his works (through chastity), and vanity (through poverty). The devil fell through the pride of disobedience, and he tempts us to go to excess in our desire for pleasure (his works) and worldly riches (vanity), and especially in our pride (disobedience). By living a truly Eucharistic life in exercising these virtues, we live out our baptismal crucifixion.

Religious obedience derives from that humility whereby we know our ignorance and need for guidance; it is that supernatural prudence of following the guidance of the Holy Spirit and those through whom the Spirit works. Obedience is more difficult and more necessary than chastity or poverty; it is the nail through the longest beam of the cross. Chastity is also a great gift of the Holy Spirit whereby we control the strongest inclinations toward pleasure and have them in proper perspective in our life. The gift of supernatural poverty enables us to evaluate and appreciate truly necessary and important possessions and to avoid the vanity, glitter, and illusions of the riches of this world. These holy nails also work to overcome the seven capital sins or, we should say, seven capital inclinations: lust, gluttony, anger, greed, vainglory, envy, and sloth.

These nails empower us to live sober, upright, and godly lives. On the moral level, our upward progress is the virtue of justice by which we give our neighbor due love and respect; on the religious level it is the virtue of religion whereby we strive to give God due worship.

While fixed on the cross of this world, our sin-prone, unstable being is held together with Christ, and we are freed to go upward, out to others and especially to the supreme Other: God. There is no nail in the upward direction. We are set free to attain true intimacy, human and divine, in self-giving love expressed through reaching out in service and worship, especially through the higher virtues of faith, hope, and love, in a contemplative spirit.

A Spiritual Cross

The cross of our human nature is a spiritual cross. It is one not of wood but of our strong fourfold inclinations. Without God's help of grace, we "would" give way to the unruly passions and desires of our weakened, fallen human nature. Without the grace of God strengthening our willpower, we go out after pleasure, possessions, and pride. Unless our unruly passions and desires are kept in check by restraining nails, we will experience a terrible existential scattering of our very being. We will become more and more like those awful beings, the *diabollein*, the torn apart, the devils, who crave to have some place to be, even dwelling in pigs.

It is our willfulness to give in to our inordinate tendencies that causes all our trouble. The cross of our being needs to be transformed from willfulness to willingness. There is no sin unless willed; likewise, there is no sanctity unless willed. The willfulness of inordinate desires needs to give way to the willingness to cooperate with the grace of God in transformation in Christ. Willingness is self-giving love; willfulness is hard-hearted selfishness. Throughout our Eucharistic life, we cooperate in our transformation in Christ by willingly renouncing our false self and living no longer for ourselves but for Jesus. That is the very reason why Jesus mounted the cross: "And he died for all, so that those who live might live no longer for themselves, but for him who died and was raised for them" (2 Cor. 5:15).

Paradoxically, to renounce self in this way is to re-announce self. As Jesus said, "Those who lose their life for my sake will find it" (Matt. 10:39). To renounce self is to proclaim one's true self in Christ, to become the transcendent self God is calling us to be. Thus, the true Christian lives a crucified life *willingly*. Living by love is a constant effort of faith, overcoming the false self and those evil spirits that are ever tempting us from the true Way. It is a daily effort to live by the spirit of poverty, chastity, and obedience that we promised at our baptism (and that some vowed in a special way at religious profession). These three spiritual nails not only save us from scattering out; they also enable us to devote our energies upward, transcending ourselves, going out to others and especially to God.

Surely the nails of love hurt and make us bleed. God wants to make us like his Son, the Way opened. The nails do just that, opening us to be a way of healing and salvation for others, as well as a means of salvation and holiness for us. True healers are wounded healers, healers who are crucified with Christ. In our spiritual life, nothing is meaningless. All the sufferings we endure throughout our Christian life are an important part of our training in self-giving love. The spiritual blood is love poured out. The nails draw forth our love for God and our neighbors. Our love becomes one with the precious redeeming love of Jesus. And we are one with him in redeeming the world.

NAILS PROMOTE THE VIRTUES

So, you see, in making our whole life a Mass, the virtues of poverty, chastity, and obedience promote our upward growth. True, we often experience them as self-denial, privation, and emptiness. But the emptiness of poverty frees us from inordinate desires for earthly possessions, from the risk of becoming possessed by our possessions, and the emptiness of chastity and obedience turns the heart to what is eternal and to greater intimacy with God.

God is our true riches and joy, the goal and satisfaction of true desire. Poverty is thus love of true wealth, the infinite riches of Christ.

Chastity purifies and strengthens our love and its expressions and helps free us from our subtle egotism and hedonism. We experience sensual pleasure less and spiritual joy more; our divided heart becomes more whole, wholesome, and able to see reality more clearly. The love that comes from a pure heart enhances prayer and true wisdom, which shows itself through doing good.

Obedience is love of the true Way, the supreme wisdom of Christ and his holy Church. It frees us from following worldly mores and strengthens our faith. Worldly prudence gradually gives way to supernatural prudence, which puts us ever more on the right way. Obedience is the victory that overcomes the world because it makes us one with the crucified Christ who has conquered the world. It purifies the soul, glorifies God, and leads to holiness. To obey is to do things God's way; it is to live Jesus, the Way.

Together these three counsels help free us daily to live the Eucharistic mystery more completely and effectively. By enhancing our faith, hope, and charity, they orient us toward contemplative living, in loving respect for our neighbor and especially our God. Without them, there are no true good works and no real contemplative prayer. Our spiritual life is a lifelong process of growth in holiness, in intimacy with God through Jesus. With good reason we live a crucified life with Christ. He is our wisdom, righteousness, sanctification, and redemption.

Breaking of Bread

From the earliest days of the Church, the Eucharist has been called the "*Breaking of Bread*." In the context of the paschal mystery, this expresses the breaking open of the way of salvation, which is Christ. As we have said, in Jesus's death his body and soul separated, like a double gate opening wide, giving all souls opportunity to enter into eternal life. The Eucharist is the Last Supper offered by Christ to perpetuate his sacrifice on the cross. Through participating in the Eucharist, all those baptized into the royal priesthood are configured more perfectly to Christ. In the *Catechism* we read:

> By giving himself to us Christ revives our love and enables us to break our disordered attachments to creatures and root ourselves in him. Since Christ died for us out of love, when we celebrate the memorial of his death at the moment of sacrifice we ask that love may be granted to us by the coming of the Holy Spirit. We humbly pray that in the strength of this love by which Christ willed to die for us, we, by receiving the gift of the Holy Spirit, may be able to consider the world as crucified for us, and to be ourselves as crucified to the world. . . . Having received the gift of love, let us die to sin and live for God. (*CCC*, 1394)

The Eucharistic sacrifice of the cross is preserved in our inmost being. It is how our life becomes a *sacrifice*, which here means "to make sacred." At Mass the mind is filled with the grace of Christ; our thinking becomes attuned to the Eucharist, with a Christlike vision of reality. It becomes easier then to recognize our risen Lord in the ups and downs of our life, and to live for Jesus and no longer for self. At Mass we mystically enter the open wounds of our Savior. We learn more and more to put off the old self of sin and to acquire our true self with Christ. The Eucharist fosters the transformation of our desires, so much so that "we have the mind of Christ" (1 Cor. 2:16). We come to desire what he desires and to think as he thinks.

Chapter 5

TEACHING THE TRUTH

"I am the truth."

—see JOHN 14:6

THE HIGHEST EDUCATION

Jesus told us that he is "the truth" (John 14:6). He revealed himself as teacher, the one and only worthy to be called teacher: "You call me Teacher and Lord—and you are right, for that is what I am" (John 13:13). "Nor are you to be called instructors, for you have one instructor, the Messiah" (Matt. 23:10). "For this I was born, and for this I came into the world, to testify to the truth" (John 18:37). "If you continue in my word, you are truly my disciples; and you will know the truth, and the truth will make you free" (John 8:31–32). His words make clear our need of this Truth. His freedom is our salvation.

Jesus's teachings are sure guides for us throughout our life. But it is above all through his Eucharistic paschal mystery that Jesus is revealed as the Truth for us. Through the Eucharist as paschal mystery, Jesus in his very being as Truth comes to us. He said, "When you have lifted up [on the cross] the Son of Man, then you will realize that I am he" (John 8:28).

Hung up naked on the cross, Jesus, the Truth, is the fullness of divine revelation lifted up on high in full display for all to see. This is something to contemplate, especially when the priest elevates the host at the consecration.

In St. John's Gospel, Jesus prays concerning the forthcoming "hour" of his crucifixion: "Father, the hour has come; glorify your Son so that the Son may glorify you" (John 17:1). We could see this glorification as a glorious explosion of Divine Truth. As we read in Hebrews, "Long ago God spoke to our ancestors in many and various ways by the prophets, but in these last days he has spoken to us by a Son" (Heb. 1:1–2). Similarly, "It is written in the prophets, 'And they shall all be taught by God.' Everyone who has heard and learned from the

Father comes to me" (John 6:45). That is the
highest education.

Through the cross Jesus comes to us in a
different way: "Even though we once knew Christ
from a human point of view, we know him no
longer in that way" (2 Cor. 5:16). At the Eucharist
we know him on the cross as the supreme Truth
of God pouring himself out in love. This pouring
out of himself happened especially in the very act
of his death. The Father's abandoning him to his
death on the cross was the dissemination of his
infinite Truth throughout the world.

The Meaning of Education

The word *education* is derived from the Latin
words *e*, meaning, "from, out of," and *duco*,
meaning "to lead, draw." Its basic meaning is a
leading or drawing out; and the result is a state
or condition into which one has been led or
drawn. Thus, education is both a process: the act
of being drawn out of ignorance into truth, and
a state: the result of one's having received and
internalized truth. This has commonly been seen
and described in terms of the drawing out of one's
potential and making it actual—as, for example,

a science student at the beginning of his studies is potentially a scientist, but only after having assimilated a good body of scientific truth do we say he is actually a scientist.

But a real education is more than receiving information; rather, it is receiving inner formation. It is the mind being formed by the truths it receives and conforming itself to the realities those truths represent. The mind is built up, matured, by those truths.

EDUCATION IN CHRIST

In viewing human nature, we discern that it is a hierarchy. What is spiritual is nobler than what is material. Thus, your soul is nobler than your body. Moreover, the soul itself, in its essence, is nobler than any of its faculties. It follows from this that there is a hierarchy of education. To educate your mind is nobler than to educate your body by building up your physical form; and, since the highest part of your being is the essence of your soul, the highest form of education is that which most directly affects that essence. Such an education elevates the very essence of your being to the level of the divine. That is where education in Christ really hits us; it is the deep work of the Holy Spirit.

The whole of the Christian life is a process of coming to know the Truth that is Christ. This process is a real education. As we have said, education is a drawing out from ignorance into truth. Jesus said that if he would be lifted up on the cross, he would draw all people to himself. He also said, "No one can come to me unless drawn by the Father who sent me" (John 6:44). This divine drawing is a mutual act of the Father and the Son, worked through the Holy Spirit of divine love, whom they send to inspire, guide, and form us into the likeness of Christ, as Jesus declared: "When the Spirit of truth comes, he will guide you into all the truth" (John 16:13).

All real education derives from and leads back to the supreme Truth that is Christ. Jesus is what the highest education is all about. St. John calls Jesus "the true light" (John 1:9). Not only is Jesus the Truth exceeding all the truths of creation, but he is also the Truth about God. Whoever knows Christ knows the Father. When the apostle Philip asked Jesus, "Lord, show us the Father, and we will be satisfied," Jesus replied, "Whoever has seen me has seen the Father" (John 14:8–9).

PERSONAL KNOWLEDGE OF CHRIST

Education in Christ is more than merely knowing Christ in concepts, more than assimilating facts about him, however lofty they may be. It is much deeper. It is intimate, direct knowledge of the very person of Jesus. He is the Truth in person, which is why he told us, "I *am* the truth." Not merely do we come to know *about* Jesus Christ; we come to intimate, unitive knowledge of the person Jesus Christ in *love*. This is true supernatural education effected by the grace of the Divine Spirit.

The most common distinctions made with respect to grace are "actual" and "sanctifying" grace. Actual grace is best understood in our context as God acting upon us, helping us and drawing us to himself. Sanctifying grace, also called habitual grace, is the transforming effect upon us when we respond properly to God's action. Actual grace can be seen as education in Christ as a process, and sanctifying grace as education in Christ as a state. As images of God, we are distorted by sin; through sanctifying grace, we are remade to the likeness of Christ in our very being. It is a permanent reality within the soul because God's offer of God's self is permanent.

MYSTICAL EDUCATION

Education in Christ is preeminently personal. Perhaps the best word to describe it is *mystical*. Every Christian possesses Christ in a mystical way, for every Christian is baptized into Christ's Mystical Body. The grace of Christ transforms us into himself. Our intimate union with him through sanctifying grace has even been called by the Fathers of the Church "divinization"—that is, becoming God by participation. It is the ultimate self-realization, the self mystically becoming one with God in Christ. Our entire Christian life and destiny can be defined as a growth in this knowledge, this union with God. The Evangelist St. John goes so far as to put this on the lips of Jesus: "And this is eternal life, that they may know you, the only true God, and Jesus Christ whom you have sent" (John 17:3).

All this begins with the great sacrament of baptism. St. Paul tells us, "As many of you as were baptized into Christ have clothed yourselves with Christ" (Gal. 3:27). Baptism is a *photismos*—that is, enlightenment with the light that is Christ. It is the beginning of a lifelong and indeed eternal process, for our intimacy with Jesus will continue and grow for all eternity, in ever-increasing union, knowledge, and joy. Here on earth we enjoy the Eucharist as this ongoing enlightenment.

With the Truth, we become truths of the faith, personal witnesses to Christ. Theologians call this the gift of justification, whereby we are made aright in the eyes of God and grow in holiness and in truth. This is truth beyond any merely intellectual truth; it is truth in being. People are right (justified) about something when they possess the truth about it.

Truth Broken Down

In his abandonment to death, Jesus was broken in body and soul. The infinite Truth of God was broken down for us to understand and was disseminated throughout the whole world. He became a life-giving spirit, transcending time and space.

The two disciples in the Emmaus story went to the apostles and told them "how he had been made known to them in the breaking of the bread" (Luke 24:35). When a lofty truth is broken down, it is made simple for even uneducated people to be able to receive and understand. It is an inestimable gift offered to all people. Jesus died for all souls. "And they shall all be taught of God" (John 6:45). Thus Jesus said, "I am the good shepherd. I know my own and my own know me" (John 10:14). To know Jesus is somehow to know all truth, for all truth is in him. Even infants can have this great knowledge because they know by experience what being loved means.

We recognize Christ especially in the Eucharistic *Breaking of Bread*. Here we experience the paschal mystery, as Jesus the lofty Truth is broken down for us. This is symbolized by the priest breaking the consecrated host and by the faithful receiving the host at Holy Communion. "[Holy] Communion . . . preserves, increases, and renews the life of grace received at Baptism" (*CCC*, 1392).

Progress in Knowledge

We experience the supreme Truth that is Christ in many ways as we live out the Mass outside of the ritual celebration. Every free moral act is either an acceptance or rejection of the offered grace of divine self-communication, the offer of Christ. Speaking to newly converted Colossians,

St. Paul declared: "You have stripped off the old self with its practices and have clothed yourselves with the new self, which is being renewed in knowledge according to the image of its creator" (Col. 3:9–10). He declared they were to "have all the riches of assured understanding and have the knowledge of God's mystery, that is, Christ himself, in whom are hidden all the treasures of wisdom and knowledge" (Col. 2:2–3).

The knowledge of Jesus sets us free with the very freedom of God. "Then Jesus said to the Jews who had believed in him, 'If you continue in my word, you are truly my disciples; and you will know the truth, and the truth will make you free'" (John 8:31–32). He went on: "So if the Son makes you free, you will be free indeed" (John 8:36).

In all forms, true freedom is freedom from the tyranny of ignorance and sin. But above all, it is freedom to do the good for which we were created, and thus to become ever more Christlike, to the honor and glory of God. St. Paul declared to Titus, "He [Jesus] it is who gave himself up for us that he might redeem us from all iniquity and purify for himself a people of his own who are zealous for good deeds" (Titus 2:14). The Truth must not merely be known but also be lived by doing good and living a virtuous life. That is to live Christ: it is making your whole life a "sacrifice of the Mass."

GROWTH IN VIRTUE

Our highest education can be seen as the acquisition of the virtues, the putting on of Christlikeness. This is the most practical level of everyday living on which we experience and can recognize in ourselves and others our education in Christ.

Living a life of virtue is to become true with the Truth and to grow into mystical union with God through Christ. The newly baptized have clothed themselves with Christ, who is Virtue personified, and the Spirit of Christ begins the glorious work of educating the soul from its innermost core. Education in Christ is learning by doing, learning at the deepest level, living the Truth that is Christ—for the Truth is a way of life to be lived. Jesus is our true vocation. "Now by this we may be sure that we know him, if we obey his commandments" (1 John 2:3).

We must be "doers of the word" (Jas. 1:22) by striving to live a truly virtuous life.

We tend to judge people as educated when they have received much schooling and seem refined, cultured, and intellectual. But such signs are really superficial and can all too easily be feigned. The surest signs of a truly educated person are gentleness and humility of heart. The proof of this is found in Jesus's words: "Take my yoke upon you, and learn from me; for I am gentle and humble in heart, and you will find rest for your souls" (Matt. 11:29). For Christians, Jesus is the Truth, and one who has learned from and about him is truly educated—has become like him. Humility and gentleness are subtle yet profound virtues that are both the foundation and the result of a life of deep spirituality.

Learning Christ Through Suffering

One important and unavoidable part of spiritual growth in virtue is suffering. Just as an athlete needs to go through the stress of training to develop his skill, so we need to endure suffering to grow in holiness. But unlike the athlete, we hardly need to seek suffering. Our loving God will send it to us, just the right amount we need at the time. Divine providence uses suffering as an important part of our education in Christ.

Suffering was viewed by the early Christians as a needed discipline and refinement of soul, a divine education. Indeed, this view was held as imitation of Christ. We read that Jesus learned obedience through suffering and was made perfect through suffering—so too for his followers in every age. Jesus urges us to take up our cross and follow him. Whoever does not is not worthy of him. We are called to share in his very sufferings, to be co-redeemers with him, to fill up what is lacking in his sufferings—the sufferings of his present Mystical Body—as did St. Paul.

We can become Christlike, not by intellectual effort, but by bearing the cross with a "love . . . that surpasses knowledge" (Eph. 3:19). Suffering out of love merits for us our heavenly home with Christ, where God will wipe away all our tears. So we willingly nail ourselves to the cross with Christ.

Suffering is not only beneficial for ourselves but also for others for whom we suffer. This is called vicarious suffering, whereby one endures suffering for the sake of others, as Jesus did.

LIGHT OF GLORY

The crucified Christ enthroned on the cross is really the glorified Christ. Before his crucifixion, Jesus prayed to his Father, "Glorify me" (John 17:1), in reference to his forthcoming paschal mystery. He did this in order to share his great glory with us. Grace is the glory radiating from the crucified Christ.

On the cross in the higher realm of divine grace, the uplifted Jesus, like the sun, is a burning and shining light, enlightening all souls of all times and places. Burning in terrible suffering on the human level—yet even more burning in life-giving love on this higher divine-human level—Jesus shines out into the darkness of our world to enlighten us with himself.

Like the sun, without which there would be no life on earth, the crucified Jesus poured himself out for and to us, and without him there would be no true spiritual and everlasting life for anyone. Only in him do we see things aright, for only he is the true light of the world of our souls. Jesus on the cross is the uplifted "sun of righteousness" (Mal. 4:2).

We marvel at pictures of the sun spewing up gigantic nuclear explosions, which propel the light and warmth by which we live. How much more should we marvel at Christ on the cross as the "sun of righteousness," pouring forth great rays of supernatural light and warmth by which we live our transcendent life of divine love?

There is a worldwide crisis in education in today's world. It is replete with terribly unbalanced opportunities for education, with poverty, and with discrimination at various levels. Even more, there is a multitude of often contradictory theories of the purposes, means, and ways of learning. These are important issues. Yet, the greatest failure is failure to realize that true education enhances life on earth but also transcends this world. We are told: "Set your minds on things that are above, not on things that are on earth" (Col. 3:2). Let us attend our next holy Mass to let the Holy Spirit draw us to Christ, the Truth, evermore.

Chapter 6

PROPAGATING LIFE

"I am the life."

—see JOHN 14:6

*"When Christ who is your life is revealed, then you
also will be revealed with him in glory."*

—COLOSSIANS 3:4

REBORN WITH CHRIST

You know the "facts of life." But do
you know the best facts of life—the
marvelous facts of the supernatural
life in Christ? Surely you do, but you need to
reflect on them again and again, as do we all.
They are so full of meaning. In this chapter, we
will look at the facts in a surprising new way,
from the viewpoint of the Holy Eucharist.

Jesus declared, "Unless you eat the flesh of the
Son of Man and drink his blood, you have no life
in you" (John 6:53). The Church teaches us that
the Eucharist is central to the life and unity of the

Church.[10] Through the Eucharist, we, the Church, the People of God, form one mystical person with Christ.

Our transcendent supernatural life is our eternal life already begun here on earth through sanctifying grace. This eternal life is our most intimate relationship in which we share in the very life of God through faith, hope, and love. It comes about in us as individual Christians through, with, and in the Eucharistic Christ. This intimacy can be seen in that we are called to be mothers of Christ, wherein the Father begets his Son in and through us. In Luke 8:21 Jesus says, "My mother and my brothers are those who hear the word of God and do it." Matthew and Mark tell us the Father's will is that we be Christ's mother: "Whoever does the will of my Father in heaven is my brother and sister and mother" (Matt. 12:50; cf. Mark 3:35). In Luke 11:27–28 Jesus stresses his spiritual sonship over his physical sonship: "A woman in the crowd raised her voice and said to him, 'Blessed is the womb that bore you and the breasts that nursed you!' But he said, 'Blessed

---

10 "The Eucharist is the efficacious sign and sublime cause of that communion in the divine life and that unity of the People of God by which the Church is kept in being" (*CCC*, 1325).

rather are those who hear the word of God and obey it.'" Mary too points to her spiritual motherhood rather than her physical one. At the very time when Mary is physically pregnant with Jesus, she cries out in her Magnificat that the Lord is magnified not by her body but by her soul: "My soul magnifies the Lord" (Luke 1:46).

So you see, according to Jesus's own words, being his spiritual mother is greater than being his physical mother. That would mean it is greater than Christmas!

Let us see how this intimate spiritual motherhood comes about in us. We saw in chapter 3 how the lofty Word of God was broken down into a tiny seed for us to receive by faith. In the parable of the sower, the seed is the word of God. In abandoning Jesus on the cross, the Father sent him out as the "imperishable seed" (1 Pet. 1:23) to yield a rich harvest for heaven. Through faith, hope, and charity, we embrace and nourish that seed in the inmost depths of our being.

The Seed-Word comes through its Sound, the Holy Spirit, and vibrates the inner ear of our heart to reproduce the Word in us and through us: "So faith comes from what is heard and what is heard comes from the word of Christ" (Rom. 10:17).

FAITH

It is with our heart that we believe—in the biblical sense of the heart as the core of the person, the deepest ground of our being and personhood whereby we are a branch of the Vine of Life. From this core comes everything to which we refer when we speak of responsibility or commitment. Faith is an act that is both exterior and interior. Faith is exterior in the conscious acceptance of the Good News as mediated through preachers, teachers, and ordinary good Christian example; faith is interior in the grace of God, which enlightens, draws, moves, and empowers the heart to acceptance and adherence. Faith never comes to an end, not even in the beatific vision: "And now faith, hope and love abide" (1 Cor. 13:13).

It is in the very act of revealing his Word to our heart that God gives us the gift of faith. In this revelation, God sows the seed of his Word in the core of our being. In accepting Jesus, we have faith. To all who accept his Word God gives the "power to become children of God" (John 1:12). As St. Paul exclaimed, "In Christ Jesus you are all children of God through faith" (Gal. 3:26).

Faith is taking God's Word for it, embracing Jesus as he comes to dwell in our heart and unite us mystically with himself. This is a powerful concept—beyond what we normally experience through the medium of natural concepts. In Jesus's dwelling within us, we experience a spiritual union greater than any physical union. By this union, we come to share the divine nature, and we become "known by God" (Gal. 4:9) in the way that he knows himself, in the very act of begetting his Son.

HOPE

There arises within us a robust hope of developing and bringing to fulfillment this radiant and holy conception. We treasure it and fix it in our memory; we draw it into the womb of our soul, which is the memory, where it attaches itself securely like an immovable anchor. There we will support, nourish, and protect it from all that could be harmful to its development.

Hope follows upon faith. "Faith is the assurance of things hoped for" (Heb. 11:1), like a seed containing what it can be when fully developed. This development is the function of hope. What is conceived by faith is kept and developed by hope. This is analogous to physical development of a child in the womb.

A pregnant woman is said to be "expecting." She is waiting patiently and joyously even in pains of pregnancy, looking forward to the birth of her child. She is full of hope. It is this hope that enables her to bear the trials of her pregnancy and to bear them even with joy. Hope is the virtue of expectancy. Through it we look forward to the fulfillment of God's great promise of salvation. We yearn to be born into eternal life with Jesus. Our calm but profoundly great excitement is one of expectation, though we rarely experience it emotionally, for it is deeper than the emotions.

The purpose of our life is to glorify God, and we do this by being "pregnant" with Christ, the Word of God. To glorify is to exalt, to magnify, to build up. A child is built up in a womb in its very being and life. Similarly, the Word of God gradually builds up within us. More and more, Jesus unfolds the richness of his heart, insofar as we open our heart to him: "Let the word of Christ dwell in you richly" (Col. 3:16).

CHARITY

What is first in intention is last in execution. All the great realities of the supernatural life are incomplete until they attain charity: love of God, neighbor, and self. St. Thomas Aquinas tells us that "faith precedes hope, and hope charity, as to their acts. . . . But in the order of perfection, charity precedes faith and hope because both faith and hope are quickened by charity, and receive from charity their full complement as virtues. For thus charity is the mother and the root of all the virtues, inasmuch as it is the form of them all."[11]

All of this is relevant to the highest facts of life, the facts of the supernatural life. In natural life the primary and most important purpose of intercourse, conception, and development of a child in a womb is to bring that child to birth. In supernatural life the primary and most important purpose of prayer, faith, and hope is rebirth with Christ in love.

11 St. Thomas Aquinas, *Summa Theologiae*, q. 62, a. 4. We note that charity is the form of all the virtues in the sense that it is their essence. Thus, faith and hope can be viewed as aspects of charity.

It is true that theologians tell us that a Christian even when he or she has lost the life of sanctifying grace and charity via mortal sin still possesses faith and hope. However, such a person possesses these in an unformed manner, because it is charity that forms all the virtues, directing and energizing each to its proper object. Hence without charity, faith and hope are possessed only in potency, just as a woman who is not pregnant still possesses the ability to conceive and bear a child. Faith and hope are not fruitful unless they are animated by charity and lead to charity as the act of giving birth.

To hear and ponder the Word of God is not enough; we must act on it. When we put the Word into practice by holy love, we are giving birth to Jesus. As Jesus said, "My mother and my brothers are those who hear the word of God and do it" (Luke 8:21).

This doing happens through the labor pangs of the spiritual life—through faithful obedience by enduring all of life's many difficulties in the love of God. St. John Paul II said, "The Church's spiritual motherhood is only achieved—the Church knows this too—through the pangs and 'the labor' of childbirth (cf. Rev 12:2), that is to say, in constant tension with the forces of evil which still roam the world and affect human hearts, offering resistance to Christ."[12]

Love is the great work of perfection. God is love. God the Father is perfect by begetting his Son, without whom he would not be *Father*. He wants to perform this great work through us. Our calling is great, very great indeed: to share in the divine nature, to share in the very act of God being God. Thus, we are forever being reborn with the eternal rebirth of the divine Son, Jesus. How magnificent is the Gospel we hear!

EUCHARISTIC ABUNDANT LIFE

In our Eucharistic worship, we are conceived with Christ by faith, developed with him in hope, and are born anew with him in charity. We must remember that, although we live the Mass in time, its reality transcends time. In the *Catechism* we read: "The Paschal mystery of Christ . . . transcends all times while being made present in them all. The event of the Cross and Resurrection *abides* and draws everything toward life" (*CCC*,

12 Pope John Paul II, *The Gospel of Life* (Boston: St. Paul Books & Media, 1995), 162.

1085). Our spiritual life with Christ is an abundant life beyond our wildest imagination.

The sacrament of the Holy Eucharist is the supreme source of charity, and growing in charity is how we live the Mass. The Spirit of God wants everything in us to bear fruit. Our faith is unfruitful and profits nothing unless we have charity: "And if I have prophetic powers, and understand all mysteries and all knowledge, and if I have all faith, so as to remove mountains, but do not have love, I am nothing" (1 Cor. 13:2). Hope is fulfilled only through God's gift of love: "And hope does not disappoint us, because God's love has been poured into our hearts through the Holy Spirit that has been given to us" (Rom. 5:5). Through the Holy Eucharist, the fruit of charity we bear is no less than Christ himself.

Chapter 7

CONTINUING THE MYSTERY

"As often as you eat this bread and drink the cup, you proclaim the Lord's death until he comes."

—1 Corinthians 11:26

The Situation Today

God continues the Eucharistic mystery in and through his Church in every era of Christianity. Through the Eucharist the mystery of redemption is carried on in which we are one with the three Divine Persons in redeeming the world. Yet all this is poorly realized and appreciated today. So, let us touch on the reality of our modern situation as best we can and probe a little more deeply into it in light of our six perspectives on the Eucharist as the ongoing paschal mystery.

Many people find the Mass boring. Why? Maybe our exasperated God is resorting to using a heavy coal-mining drill to bore through the hardness of their hearts, as he promised "I will remove from your body the heart of stone" (Ezek. 36:26). Many older people have had their hearts broken open through suffering—a big advantage over the young—so it is no surprise to see more older folks at Mass. But mostly it is a matter of simple economics. If we find Mass boring, we may not have invested enough of ourselves spiritually to gain much interest. We are bored when we lack interest and attention. We "pay" attention. Attention is the currency of the mind; it's what we spend to obtain knowledge and love. The amount of interest we gain on an investment depends on how much currency we invest in it. We need to act on our faith in everyday living, in order to gain the power, attitude, and motivation to increase our attention and interest.

The Mass is not entertainment. It will never be as exciting as your favorite team's last-second winning goal. But attendance at Mass is never fruitless, even when we are bored; we must remember that God's grace affects us especially in our depths, beyond our consciousness. At least the bored are present, and that is saying something. Indeed, isn't it much to their merit that they persevere in their boredom? Attentive participation means to recite when we are supposed to recite, to sing when we are called to sing, and especially to pray internally throughout. Through this participation, you invest the currency of your mind and gain great interest. And you store up into your heavenly account vast riches that you will enjoy when you cash in your earthly life.

Neither is the Mass magic. It is not based on trickery but on truth. The Eucharist is a sacrament instituted by Christ to unite himself with us in ever more complete intimacy. Since the sacraments are God's sacred signs that remind us of Christ, they all flow from the Eucharist, of which Jesus said, "Do this in remembrance of me" (Luke 22:19).

Above all, the Mass is prayer. We proclaim Jesus, the infinitely perfect Word of prayer. To the Father, we offer the glorifying Word; and to the world, we offer the sanctifying Word: worship and evangelization. And this Word profoundly affects us. Through the Eucharist we become, with Christ, ever more powerful words of prayer—individually and as a community in Christ—and this transforms everything we do, for we do it through, with, and in Jesus. Jesus is our Word of prayer in all of its four dimensions: adoration, thanksgiving, petition, and repentance.[13] The more truly we live the Mass, the more we become powerful words of prayer with Christ. We can "pray always" (1 Thess. 5:17) in our Eucharistic life of self-giving love.

THE FULLNESS OF EXPERIENCE

At Mass, we can experience all six views of the paschal mystery that we have pondered. There the Word of the Cross is proclaimed: Christ, the Gospel. If somehow the Eucharist were eliminated from the earth, there would be no Gospel, no faith, and no salvation. St. Paul exclaimed, "As often as you eat this bread and drink the cup, you proclaim the Lord's death until he comes" (1 Cor. 11:26). This is a divine as well as a human proclamation. The death of the Lord *is* the proclamation of the Word. It is the Father and Son proclaiming the Word, re-announcing Jesus—the Father in a divine way and Jesus in a human way, as we saw in chapter 1.

13 Some examples from Scripture of Christ as Prayer in the four dimensions of prayer are the following: Heb. 13:15, adoration; Eph. 5:20, thanksgiving; Heb. 7:25, intercession; 1 John 2:2, repentance.

Note that St. Paul said "*you* proclaim"; *you* are proclaiming with God the divine-human Word! Your role is vital; this proclamation takes place especially in the eating of Christ's body and drinking of his blood. This is not all passive. You eat and drink, a great act of faith in love. In the Eucharist, you re-member Christ, putting together the dis-membered, sin-broken, "made-sin" Word.

Pope Francis urged all of us: "Evangelizing is the Church's mission. It is not the mission of only a few, but it is mine, yours and our mission. The Apostle Paul exclaimed: 'woe to me if I do not preach the Gospel' (1 Cor 9:16). We must all be evangelizers, especially with our life!"[14]

God the Father exists to proclaim his Word in the Spirit of love, and we participate in this through our Eucharistic proclamation. We execute the Truth in love. This is, as it were, the opposite of Calvary. The Eucharistic proclamation is life-giving rather than life-taking. We give new life to Jesus in our hearts, where he delights to dwell.

The Eucharistic memorial is the release of the infinite Power of God (see chapter 2), the source of all divine grace. By grace we are empowered to

14 Pope Francis, General Audience, May 22, 2013.

live Christ in a virtuous life and to help others to do so. Our hearts are set ablaze by the Eucharistic paschal mystery, and we become a part of the great explosion of love, as an ever new creation in Christ.

We are one with God in re-membering humankind in the Mystical Body of Christ, in the overcoming of sin (see chapter 3). The blood of the Eucharist is the blood "poured out for many for the forgiveness of sins" (Matt. 26:28). At the Eucharist we offer Christ to the Father as payment that more than satisfies for all human sins, reconciles us with God, and makes the People of God one.

Here let us recall our being nailed to the cross with Christ by our self-denial (see chapter 4). The spirit of self-denial is profoundly exercised at Mass. For example, our senses tell us this is bread, but we say it is the body of Christ; our senses say this is wine, but we say it is the blood of Christ. Someone could say, "You are out of your mind! You are denying your senses." We could answer, "Yes, we are out of our mind, because in faith we live by the mind of Christ, not our own." We are *all the more* in line with reality. We are better able to face and find meaning in the challenges and sufferings of life. In our humble prayer at Mass, we look in contemplation on the "one whom [we] have pierced" (John 19:37), the opened Way to eternal life. Christ is drawing us to himself through his great Eucharistic graces in our highest education (see chapter 5).

The earliest Christians met on Sundays to break bread, and the Eucharist remains at the center of Church life today.[15] We recognize the Lord in the Eucharistic *Breaking of Bread,* whereby Jesus is given to us by our loving God, "who desires everyone to be saved and to come to the knowledge of the truth" (1 Tim. 2:4).

Through the Mass we grow in Christ and become sources of life for others by fostering faith, hope, and charity (see chapter 6). We realize that the Eucharist is the "mystery of faith" whereby we conceive the Word of God and are conceived with the Word. The Eucharist is the source of Christian life.

---

15 "From that time on down to our own day the celebration of the Eucharist has been continued so that today we encounter it everywhere in the Church with that same structure. It remains the center of the Church's life" (*CCC*, 1343).

Paschal Mystery in the Flow of the Mass

Now let us examine the structure of the Mass. We will see how the Eucharist is the paschal mystery in an overall way by understanding the two parts of the Mass—the Liturgy of the Word and the Liturgy of the Eucharist—and its three main actions: offertory, consecration, and communion.

We see these three actions in the paschal mystery. Even anticipating the terrible sufferings of the Cross, Jesus offered himself to the Father in the Garden of Gethsemane. Then at the moment of death on the cross, he cried out, "Father, into your hands I commend my spirit" (Luke 23:46), in total self-giving love. With him, at the Eucharist we offer ourselves to God in the same Spirit. Through the paschal mystery, Jesus was consecrated like the bread and wine at Mass, becoming a "new man." He consecrates himself so we can be consecrated in him. Finally, bringing about communion of souls with God in and through himself is the whole intent of his paschal mystery, "that all may be one" (John 17:21).

The structure of the Mass reflects and enhances our encounter with God. From the introductory rite through the Liturgy of the Word, we acknowledge that we are the People of God in Christ, gathered in adoration and praise. This praise is especially seen in the Gloria, but also throughout the Mass. Included are acts of petition, repentance, and thanksgiving, all as appropriate throughout the ceremony. Without doubt our heavenly Father is delighted when, early on in the penitential rite, we confess sorrow for our sins, for then we are completing his merciful act of forgiveness. Forgiveness is not complete until the guilty one acknowledges his or her guilt in sorrow.

Then we come to the Liturgy of the Word, in which the Father abandons to us his divine-human Word to instruct us in the Truth, especially through our listening to Holy Scripture and the homily. Jesus enters more profoundly into our hearts, is written more deeply in our depths; we receive a renewed spirit.

In the Profession of Faith we give further assent to what we have heard in the readings and the homily and summarize the teachings of the Faith in the creed before we celebrate the Eucharist. Then, moved by God's Word, we petition for the needs of God's people and of the whole world in the General Intercessions. With our hearts made purer by his Word, we can call on the Lord.

Now comes the Liturgy of the Eucharist, of thanksgiving, in which we are one with Christ in gratitude for God's many blessings. With Jesus, the Word of petition, we make our petitions; with Jesus, the Word of thanks, we give our thanks. With Christ, the priest, we exercise our baptismal priesthood in the Eucharistic Prayer, rejoicing in God's great work of redemption. All this occurs in the Holy Spirit. Called down upon the altar at the Epiclesis, the Holy Spirit is the powerful Sound of the Word hovering over the congregation to form us into the new creation in Christ. The Spirit's presence is profoundly social as well as deeply personal in the heart of each participant. The liturgy thus is a paschal movement of new creation from the Father, through the Son, and in the Spirit.

The Liturgy of the Eucharist begins with the Offertory, where we offer ourselves to God with Christ.[16] We praise the Blessed Trinity: "Holy, Holy, Holy." Then follows the consecration of

16 "They [Christ's faithful] should give thanks to God; offering the Immaculate Victim, not only through the hands of the priest, but also with him, they should learn also to offer themselves" (*Sacrosanctum Concilium*, 48).

the bread and wine into the body and blood of Christ, and we proclaim the "mystery of faith" and proceed to the Communion rite.

The consecration and Communion necessarily go together, for the transformation of the bread and wine are meant to lead to the salvific and sanctifying transformation of God's people. God is not changed, and Christ is not changed; we are changed. The Communion rite includes the Our Father, the sign of peace, and the priest's breaking of the bread. Then we proclaim Jesus as the Lamb of God, which expresses his sacrificial character as well as his innocence, gentleness, and triumph on the cross. Next we receive him in Holy Communion.

In the final part of the Mass, after the priest blesses us, we are sent forth on our mission to go and make our entire life a "holy sacrifice of the Mass." The priest tells us, *Ite, missa est*—"Go, you are sent forth."

Chapter 8

REMEMBERING JESUS

"Do this in remembrance of me."

—LUKE 22:19

A LITERAL INTERPRETATION

Our appreciation of the Eucharist would be seriously incomplete if we did not look on it as a memorial. In fact, we should view it as "the" memorial of Jesus because only of it did Jesus say, "Do this in remembrance of me" (Luke 22:19).

Unfortunately, the Eucharist as a memorial is poorly understood and appreciated. Most Christians, including theologians and liturgists, interpret Jesus's words, "Do this in remembrance of me," by which he instituted the sacrament, in an exclusively natural way. They treat the act of remembering in this sacrament as they would any natural act of memory. When striving to teach of the importance and benefits of this remembering, they fall back on understandings of the value of memory in human life. This is all well and good as far as it goes, but it does not go far enough; indeed it is woefully lacking. There is far more to the Eucharist as a memorial than that.

There is also the question of who does the remembering. Like most Christians, you probably believe that it is you who do it, and that indeed seems justified not only by the common approach to the Eucharist but also by the implied addition of "you" in text itself: *you* do this in remembrance of me. However, as we shall see, the text can have other forms of meaning.

We need to take Jesus's words of institution at face value; we need to interpret them literally. Jesus did not say, "Do this in remembrance of my passion, death, and resurrection," or any such words. He said, "Do this in remembrance of *me*." The Eucharist is a recollecting of Jesus. It is not merely our recalling his earthly life, thoughts, words, and deeds, no matter how wonderful that may be. The Eucharist is literally the recalling of the person, Jesus. And it is not merely a human recalling of Jesus but a divine recalling, whereby Jesus himself becomes present. The key to understanding this is to realize that the words "do this in remembrance of me" are being said by the Word of God. The Eucharist is a recalling of that Word of God; as such, it is a rich mystery with infinite depth of meaning for us.

In this book we have seen that the Annunciation was the calling of the Word of God to earth, and the paschal mystery is the re-calling of the Word of God in a new and glorious way, in his humanity. The first was an emptying, the second a fulfilling. This brings to mind the great hymn in Philippians 2 referring to the act whereby God "emptied himself" (Phil. 2:7) and became a man. And in the Letter to the Hebrews 2:10, we read that Jesus was made perfect through his sufferings that brought about his death.

Moreover, the paschal mystery is not only the perfect human fulfillment of Jesus, but also the true and glorious fulfillment of ourselves, God's sons and daughters. The Eucharistic recollecting, which is the paschal mystery, is the ongoing new creation in Christ in which he leads souls to salvation. The Eucharist is what keeps the Church in being, as the *ecclesia*, the assembly of God's people called together as one for the eternal glory of God.

In His Redeeming Act

In being remembered in the Liturgy of the Eucharist, Christ becomes present in his salvific death, symbolized by the separate consecration of the bread and wine. In the Mass we hear the priest say, "Take this, all of you, and eat it. This is my body which will be *given* up for you." With these words, Christ's body is *given*, as dead to this world yet glorified and alive to God. "This is the cup of my blood, the blood of the new and everlasting covenant. It will be *shed* for you and for all men"—that is, Jesus's blood poured out in death. He is present in the redeeming act of his death, memorialized in the Eucharist.

In the Eucharist, Christ is present to us and for us, but also *with* us; he is present to share his act of redeeming the world with us, to give us a real participation in it. Mystically we die Christ's death to sin and are alive to God with him. Moreover, there is one bread, and we all form one body in Christ—we the Church become the very body of the Lord in his redeeming act. By his resurrection, he dies no more but is a heavenly reality, transcending time and space. Through his Holy Spirit, we call him down at Mass.

As we proceed in this chapter, let us try to realize the richness of this great memorial of Jesus, the ritual act of the Mass and our living it out in our lives.

RECALLING JESUS

The Eucharist is *the* recalling of Jesus. As we have noted, only of it did Jesus say, "Do *this* in remembrance of me." In chapters 1 and 2 we saw something of God's powerful calling of his Word. At Mass we proclaim the death of the Lord, which death *is* the proclamation of the Word, as we have maintained. This proclamation, this call, is the highest meaning of the Gospel. But note that while in the Eucharist we recall the Word, the Eucharist is effective above all through God's act of recalling his Word. It is a mutual recalling. Vatican II told us that when the Church is proclaiming the Word of God, Christ is still proclaiming his gospel (see *Sacrosanctum Concilium*, 33). Jesus, the divine-human Word of God, is proclaiming himself in and through us, his Mystical Body. He is one with his heavenly Father in sending forth the divine Sound of the Word, empowering us to live a life of virtue.

Scripture scholar Joachim Jeremias tells us that Luke 22:19 can also be translated: "Do this that God may remember me."[17] A word is resurrected by being recalled. When God re-calls Christ, he calls out anew in the most perfect way, resurrecting his Word.

But, you may object, that implies that when Jesus died he was forgotten by God. Does God forget? What could that mean? Maybe an answer lies in the fact that at his death Jesus descended into hell. Hell in Old Testament times was known as Sheol, the "land of forgetfulness" (Ps. 88:12). It is a place where the dead are no longer remembered, even by Yahweh. "[I am] like those whom you remember no more" (Ps. 88:5).

Based on our knowledge of the Trinity, we could perhaps speculate as follows. When we look at the Eucharist as a memorial through God's action, the Eucharist is his raising up of the crucified Jesus from the dead, the ongoing eternal reality of Jesus as the Resurrection. This mirrors the eternal act of the Father begetting his Son, who, as the Resurrection, is the abundant

17 Joachim Jeremias, *The Eucharistic Words of Jesus* (Norwich, UK: Hymns Ancient & Modern, 2012), 254–55. He goes on to tell us that God's remembering is always an effecting and creative event, 248.

life ever rising up to life, the Word ever being proclaimed in the Sound of the Spirit. The Father is ever calling forth his Word again and again—re-calling the Word. Thus the Eucharist is the ongoing resurrection of Jesus; it is the Father re-calling Jesus, calling him out in the Sound of the Holy Spirit as the Word of salvation to be reborn in and through us.

When we look at the Eucharist as also our action, it is our participation in God's act. A counterpart of the resurrection of Jesus is our participation in God's act of giving Jesus to us to live in our hearts through faith—to be our true life, our true vocation. We could say that Jesus resurrects mystically within the world of our soul. Every holy Mass brings an increase in faith and thus a greater union with Jesus, a greater remembering of him in our hearts. We recall Christ insofar as we live the Mass by making our life a sacrifice of love. More than merely recalling Jesus mentally, by every good act we re-call him and remind others of him, for everything we do, we do with him. Jesus lived all his mysteries on earth only so that he could live them over again in us, to our great benefit.

This is the marvelous re-calling of the whole Mystical Body of Christ—as members of his Mystical Body, we too are re-called, called out anew as words of divine praise and adoration, rooted in Christ. We were incorporated into Christ—as words derived from the Word—at the moment of our baptism. Throughout our entire lives, we are ever being called back—re-called—from our sinful ways: repentant, called out anew, transformed in Christ, as a new creation. We proclaim Christ by every good act we do as we progress along the Way of love. Insofar as we imitate Christ, we are synonyms of the Word.

Remembered in Christ

The Eucharist is the great sacrament of unity; it is God establishing his new covenant with his people. The communal aspect of the Eucharist is indispensable. Broken, dis-membered, sinful souls are being re-membered, put together anew in Christ. True love unites. The individual grows in true unity of being, true personal integrity, wholeness of life and being—from being scattered in sin to being whole (holy) in grace. The word *salvation* implies this wholeness.

Likewise, in humankind there is the ongoing increase of the kingdom of God. There is the growth of the Church, the Mystical Body of Christ, the redemption of the world—that all may be one as the Father and Son are one in the Spirit. Through the Eucharist there is the ongoing creation in Christ, the ever-increasing coming of the kingdom. We are mindful here of what we said in chapters 3 and 4, that sinful souls are healed by entry into the open way by baptism, through which we are re-membered within Christ's Mystical Body, the Church. This is continued in the sacrament of reconciliation whereby our subsequent sins are wiped away.

The three Divine Persons as being-in-communion sustain all of creation in a life of communion. Created in the image and likeness of God, we are called to be beings in communion: to live out our baptismal commitment via the Eucharist and to realize our true personhood through a life of communion with God and one another.

This graced encounter occurs especially in our reception of Christ in Holy Communion. This is far from being merely a singular personal encounter—it enhances our spiritual growth in union with all God's people. We are empowered by grace to move selflessly toward others—in openness, trust, and vulnerability—seeking their good for its own sake rather than our own ends. In short, we are to be church, the assembly of the People of God. Holy Communion is inseparable from our communion with our neighbor.

This re-membering of sinful souls is the proper work of the Holy Spirit, who is divine love. Communally, the Mystical Body of Christ led by the Holy Spirit forms the true history of God's people, written in heaven as well as on earth— words poured forth in glorious divine praise. On the personal level, in and through the Holy Spirit we achieve a wholeness, which is holiness. Our good God calls us to this wholeness in the first and greatest of his commandments: "Love the LORD your God with all your heart, and with all your soul, and with all your might" (Deut. 6:5).

REMINDED OF CHRIST

St. Paul urged: "Do not be conformed to this world, but be transformed by the renewing of your minds, so that you may discern what is the will of God—what is good and acceptable and perfect" (Rom. 12:2). Such a transformed person is crucified with Christ, dead to the false self, and lives no longer for self but for Christ. He or she has been re-minded of Christ.

By God's grace we are being transformed, putting on the mind of Christ—his outlook on life and reality, his values, his desires. We become a new self. This occurs deep down beyond the level of conscious thought, in that dimension of our soul that is the source of all our intellectual activity, imagination, intuition, and moral choices. This spiritual transformation is our education in Christ, which we discussed in chapter 5.

This re-minding involves, not a matter of objective knowledge, but a sense of self-awareness as well as intensified awareness of the presence of God. We experience it more concretely, for example, in changed attitudes, in our judgments of truth, and in our judgments of value. We come more and more to see life and reality as Jesus does, in holy love, rather than with our limited attitudes, judgments, and opinions.

In this transformation we become more like Jesus from glory to glory. Thus St. Paul could proclaim that "we have the mind of Christ" (1 Cor. 2:16). This transformation is lifelong because we can never become Christ-minded enough. It is life-giving as we grow in faith, hope, and charity, as we discussed in chapter 6. More and more we seek the things that are above rather than of earth. More and more we come to see everything in this life on earth in the perspective of eternity. This leads to and enhances purity of heart; our unruly passions and desires come under greater control, harmony, and purification, better able to be at the service of love.

Eucharist Extended

The power of the Eucharist extends throughout the sacramental system; we can see each of the other six sacraments as extensions of the sacrament of the Eucharist. The six views of the Eucharist we have contemplated bear this out. Each points to one of the other sacraments, for all the others flow from the Eucharist and look back to it. As the "source and summit of the Christian life" (*CCC*, 1324), the Eucharist is the source and summit of the sacramental system.

From the perspective of proclaiming the Word (chapter 1), there flows the sacrament of holy orders. At the paschal mystery Jesus was changed into a life-giving spirit. Men are ordained to change bread and wine into Jesus's body and blood, to bring about his presence in an especially real way. And they are ordained to bring about Jesus's presence through their preaching. "Releasing Power" (chapter 2) points to the sacrament of anointing of the sick; it imparts life-giving spiritual power, which can at times overflow into physical power and healing.

In chapter 3, "Overcoming Sin," we can see the sacrament of reconciliation, in which our sins are forgiven. In our fourth viewpoint, "Opening the Way," we recognize our incorporation into Christ at baptism, our being welcomed into the open way whereby we became a member of Christ's Mystical Body, the Church. The sacrament of confirmation flows from our fifth perspective, "Teaching the Truth," in which our supreme education in Christ can be received in a sacramental way when a child is mature enough to understand and appreciate his or her Christian role and responsibilities in life. Finally, chapter 6, "Propagating Life," points to the sacrament of holy matrimony.

There is much food for thought in these holy proceedings from the Eucharist, and there is no better way to understand and appreciate each sacrament than by contemplating it in relation to the Eucharist, its source and orientation.

THE LAST WORD

Because God is the highest good, God is also our greatest joy, for the good is the object of love and love leads to joy. The experience of joy is the result of loving and being loved. The Holy Spirit, by pouring love into our hearts, sets us on the way to everlasting joy. Ultimately this is experienced in the beatific vision in heaven. But our Christian life on earth is not without joy and love; they are the firstfruits of the Holy Spirit.

The Holy Spirit plants desire for joy and love in the core of our hearts, for God wants to make us like himself. Destined for everlasting joy in a life of love, we know that neither suffering nor death nor the cross will have the last word. Nothing can separate us from the love of Christ. Insofar as we remain in Christ through a faithful life of self-giving love, we will come to experience the fullness of joy. All of the mysteries associated with the paschal mystery are means to that never-ending joy of being ever more Eucharistically re-called, re-minded, and re-membered by, with, and to God. And what is the beatific vision and communion of saints all about if not re-calling God's Word, re-minding God of God, and re-membering souls in Christ?

The Crucifixion is still going on through the suffering of the people of God: Christ's Mystical Body, the Church. Like St. Paul, all souls are called to complete what is lacking in the sufferings of Christ. In his tremendous love for us, God has left his work of redemption incomplete so we can participate through our good works, trials, and prayers. Through Christ, God is calling us all to be co-redeemers in intimate union with the Blessed Trinity.

Thus, the work of redemption goes on. It must continue until the kingdom of God has been fully established on earth as God desires it to be. Our Eucharistic communion with Christ must bear fruit in good works. By each of us fulfilling our particular mission in life through making our whole life a holy Mass in self-giving love, we foster the work of redemption. This work of redemption is the work of saving souls for heaven. It is the height of divine praise on earth and is manifested in evangelization and divine worship. There is no more important work.

ABOUT PARACLETE PRESS

Who We Are

Paraclete Press is a publisher of books, recordings, and DVDs on Christian spirituality. Our publishing represents a full expression of Christian belief and practice—from Catholic to Evangelical, from Protestant to Orthodox.

We are the publishing arm of the Community of Jesus, an ecumenical monastic community in the Benedictine tradition. As such, we are uniquely positioned in the marketplace without connection to a large corporation and with informal relationships to many branches and denominations of faith.

What We Are Doing

PARACLETE PRESS BOOKS

Paraclete publishes books that show the richness and depth of what it means to be Christian. Although Benedictine spirituality is at the heart of all that we do, we publish books that reflect the Christian experience across many cultures, time periods, and houses of worship. We publish books that nourish the vibrant life of the church and its people.

We have several different series, including the best-selling Paraclete Essentials and Paraclete Giants series of classic texts in contemporary English; Voices from the Monastery—men and women monastics writing about living a spiritual life today; award-winning poetry; best-selling gift books for children on the occasions of baptism and first communion; and the Active Prayer Series that brings creativity and liveliness to any life of prayer.

MOUNT TABOR BOOKS

Paraclete's newest series, Mount Tabor Books, focuses on liturgical worship, art and art history, ecumenism, and the first millennium church, and was created in conjunction with the Mount Tabor Ecumenical Centre for Art and Spirituality in Barga, Italy.

PARACLETE RECORDINGS

From Gregorian chant to contemporary American choral works, our recordings celebrate the best of sacred choral music composed through the centuries that create a space for heaven and earth to intersect. Paraclete Recordings is the record label representing the internationally acclaimed choir Gloriæ Dei Cantores, praised for their "rapt and fathomless spiritual intensity" by *American Record Guide*; the Gloriæ Dei Cantores Schola, specializing in the study and performance of Gregorian chant; and the other instrumental artists of the Gloriæ Dei Artes Foundation.

Paraclete Press is also privileged to be the exclusive North American distributor of the recordings of the Monastic Choir of St. Peter's Abbey in Solesmes, France, long considered to be a leading authority on Gregorian chant.

PARACLETE VIDEO

Our DVDs offer spiritual help, healing, and biblical guidance for a broad range of life issues including grief and loss, marriage, forgiveness, facing death, bullying, addictions, Alzheimer's, and spiritual formation.

Learn more about us at our website:
www.paracletepress.com
or phone us toll-free at 1.800.451.5006

SCAN
TO
READ
MORE

YOU MIGHT ALSO BE INTERESTED IN

Freedom and Forgiveness
A Fresh Look at the Sacrament of Reconciliation
Fr. Paul Farren

$8.99 PAPERBACK,
ISBN 978-1-61261-498-4

Fr. Paul describes reconciliation as God's gift to us to express God's humble forgiveness and his confidence in us and also the place where we take responsibility for our lives.

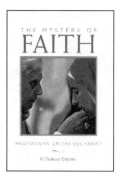

The Mystery of Faith
Meditations on the Eucharist
Fr. Tadeusz Dajczer

$17.99 HARDCOVER,
ISBN 978-1-55725-686-7

We want to live the Eucharist, not just go to Mass, and here is a clear and compassionate voice of encouragement.

Available from most booksellers or through Paraclete Press:
WWW.PARACLETEPRESS.COM | 1-800-451-5006
Try your local bookstore first.